Lemurs

Lemurs

Mary Ann McDonald

THE CHILD'S WORLD®, INC.

Library of Congress Cataloging-in-Publication Data
McDonald, Mary Ann.
Lemurs / by Mary Ann McDonald.
p.   cm.
Includes index.
Summary: Describes the physical characteristics,
behavior, habitat, and life cycle of the lemur.
ISBN 1-56766-495-4 (lib. bdg. : alk paper)
1. Lemurs—Juvenile literature.
[1. Lemurs.]   I. Title.
QL737.P95M393   1998
599.8'3—dc21   97-44649
                              CIP
                              AC

Photo Credits

© Alan and Sandy Carey: cover, 2, 16, 20, 29, 30
ANIMALS ANIMALS © David Haring: 24
© Joe McDonald: 6, 9, 13, 15, 19, 23
© S. Cordier/Jacana, The National Audubon Society Collection/PR: 10
© Tom McHugh, The National Audubon Society Collection/PR: 26

On the cover...

Front cover: This *ring-tailed lemur* is playing on the ground.
Page 2: This *black and white lemur* is climbing down a tree.

Table of Contents

In a thick forest on a faraway island, you can see and hear many animals. Some walk along near huge plants. Others swoop and soar over the green trees. But high in the treetops, a strange animal leaps from branch to branch. What could this weird animal be? It's a lemur!

⇐ This young ring-tailed lemur is playing on a branch.

What Are Lemurs?

Lemurs belong to a family of animals called **primates**. Primates are very smart. They also use their hands to feed themselves. Gorillas, chimpanzees, and people are primates, too. Lemurs are not as highly developed as other kinds of primates. Once lemurs lived throughout the world. Now they live only on the islands of Madagascar and Comoro.

This *crowned lemur* is watching some other lemurs. ⇒

What Do Lemurs Look Like?

Lemurs come in many different sizes. The biggest lemur is the *indri.* It is about the size of a dog. The smallest lemur is called the *lesser mouse lemur.* It is only as big as a mouse.

All lemurs have soft fur that covers most of their bodies. Some have long, pointed noses, too. Many lemurs have bushy tails as long as their bodies. Others have no tails at all.

⇐ This *lesser-mouse lemur* is keeping an eye out for danger.

Where Do Lemurs Like to Live?

Lemurs are **arboreal**, which means that they live mostly in trees. They eat, play, sleep and even have their babies high in the treetops. Lemurs get around easily by climbing and leaping from branch to branch. Some kinds of lemurs can even leap to branches 20 feet away!

This *gentle bamboo lemur* is hiding in some thick branches. ⇒

Some lemurs are **nocturnal**, which means that they are active only at night. They spend the day sleeping in hollow trees. Other lemurs are **diurnal**—they are active during the day. Diurnal lemurs look for food during the day and sleep in the trees at night.

Coquerel's Sifaka lemurs like this one are diurnal. ⇒

Lemurs eat lots of fruits and leaves. They also eat tree bark, buds, flowers, nuts, roots, insects, and sometimes young birds. Some lemurs, such as the *mongoose lemur*, also lick the sweet liquid that flowers produce. This liquid is called **nectar**.

⇐ This *mongoose lemur* is eating some juicy leaves.

The *aye-aye* is an insect-eating lemur that finds its dinner in an unusual way. Aye-ayes have a very long middle finger. The aye-aye taps this finger along branches and listens for a hollow sound. A hollow sound means there is a hidden hole made by a young insect. The aye-aye uses its sharp teeth to open up the hole. Then it uses its long finger to find the insect, hook onto it, and bring it out for dinner.

If you look closely, you can see this *aye-aye's* long middle finger. ⇒

Nocturnal lemurs like to live alone. Diurnal lemurs live in small groups Each group defends its area of land against other groups. Some lemur groups are made up of just one family. Others consist of several females and males with their young.

Are Lemurs Active All Year?

During the dry times of the year, lemurs sometimes have a hard time finding enough to eat. *Dwarf lemurs* and *mouse lemurs* survive this difficult time by going into a deep sleep. Just before the dry season, they eat huge amounts of food. This food helps them build up body fat that they store in their tails. They live off this fat during their long, deep sleep. When it is time to find food again, the lemurs finally wake up.

⇐ This *greater mouse lemur* is eating a flower.

Lemurs that sleep during the dry season also go into a deep sleep when the weather gets too cold. In other parts of the world, many other animals go into this cold-weather sleep. It is the only way they can survive the long winters. An animal's deep winter sleep is called *hibernation*.

Are Lemurs in Danger?

The greatest danger to lemurs is the loss of the forests in which they live. The forests of Madagascar are being destroyed more and more each year. Many large areas have already been burned to make room for grazing and farming. Without the forests, lemurs are having a hard time finding enough food to eat and places to sleep and play.

These mongoose lemurs are in danger of losing their forest home. ⇒

There is some hope for the animals and plants that live in these forests. Many schools are now teaching children about preserving nature. Children are learning that forests all over the world are important for many reasons. If people work together to save the world's forests, we will be able to enjoy the delightful lemurs for a long time.

Glossary

arboreal (ar–BOR–ee–ull)
Arboreal animals live in trees. Lemurs are arboreal.

diurnal (dy–UR–null)
A diurnal animal sleeps at night and moves around during the day. People are diurnal, and so are some lemurs.

nectar (NEK–ter)
The sweet liquid made by flowers is called nectar. Some lemurs like to eat nectar.

nocturnal (nok–TUR–null)
Nocturnal animals move around at night and sleep during the day. Some lemurs are nocturnal.

primates (PRY–mates)
Primates are a group of animals that are very intelligent and use their hands to feed themselves and for other tasks. People, monkeys, apes, and lemurs are all primates.

Index